Fortinet Network Security Expert 4 (NSE4 FGT 6.2) Exam Practice Questions & Dumps

Exam Practice Questions for NSE4 FGT 6.2
LATEST VERSION

Presented by: Quantic Books

About Quantic Books:

Quantic Books is a publishing house based in Princeton, New Jersey, USA. , a platform that is accessible online as well as locally, which gives power to educational content, erudite collection, poetry & many other book genres. We make it easy for writers & authors to get their books designed, published, promoted, and sell professionally on worldwide scale with eBook + Print distribution. Quantic Books is now distributing books worldwide.

Note: Find answers of the questions at the last of the book.

QUESTION 1

Which statement about FortiGuard services for FortiGate is true?

A. The web filtering database is downloaded locally on FortiGate.
B. Antivirus signatures are downloaded locally on FortiGate.
C. FortiGate downloads IPS updates using UDP port 53 or 8888.
D. FortiAnalyzer can be configured as a local FDN to provide antivirus and IPS updates.

QUESTION 2

Which of the following route attributes must be equal for static routes to be eligible for equal cost multipath (ECMP) routing? (Choose two.)

A. Priority
B. Metric
C. Distance
D. Cost

QUESTION 3

View the exhibit.

```
Local-FortiGate # diagnose sys ha checksum cluster
================== FGVM010000058290 ==================

is_manage_master()=1, is_root_master()=1
debugzone
global: 85 26 52 f2 f9 6e 3c c9 f5 21 1a 78 69 b6 20 bd
root: 30 51 63 1b 2d ef 77 aa f7 50 00 25 4d 42 a9 7d
all: 38 28 3d e4 24 8f 5b 10 8a 64 30 f2 34 13 c1 35

checksum
global: 85 26 52 f2 f9 6e 3c c9 f5 21 1a 78 69 b6 20 bd
root: 30 51 63 1b 2d ef 77 aa f7 50 00 25 4d 42 a9 7d
all: 38 28 3d e4 24 8f 5b 10 8a 64 30 f2 34 13 c1 35

================== FGVM010000058289 ==================

is_manage_master()=0, is_root_master()=0
debugzone
global: 85 26 52 f2 f9 6e 3c c9 f5 21 1a 78 69 b6 20 bd
root: 30 51 63 1b 2d ef 77 aa f7 50 00 25 4d 8a 55 8b
all: 38 28 3d e4 24 8f 5b 10 8a 64 30 f2 34 dc 9a 43

checksum
global: 85 26 52 f2 f9 6e 3c c9 f5 21 1a 78 69 b6 20 bd
root: 30 51 63 1b 2d ef 77 aa f7 50 00 25 4d 8a 55 8b
all: 38 28 3d e4 24 8f 5b 10 8a 64 30 f2 34 dc 9a 43
```

Based on this output, which statements are correct? (Choose two.)

A. The `all` VDOM is not synchronized between the primary and secondary FortiGate devices.

B. The `root` VDOM is not synchronized between the primary and secondary FortiGate devices.

C. The global configuration is synchronized between the primary and secondary FortiGate devices.

D. The FortiGate devices have three VDOMs.

QUESTION 4

Which statement is true regarding the policy ID number of a firewall policy?

A. Defines the order in which rules are processed.
B. Represents the number of objects used in the firewall policy.
C. Required to modify a firewall policy using the CLI.
D. Changes when firewall policies are reordered.

QUESTION 5

An administrator wants to block HTTP uploads. Examine the exhibit, which contains the proxy address created for that purpose.

Where must the proxy address be used?

A. As the source in a firewallpolicy.
B. As the source in a proxy policy.
C. As the destination in a firewall policy.
D. As the destination in a proxy policy.

QUESTION 6

Which statement is true regarding SSL VPN timers? (Choose two.)

A. Allow to mitigate DoS attacks from partial HTTP requests.
B. SSL VPN settings do not have customizable timers.
C. Disconnect idle SSL VPN users when a firewall policy authentication timeout occurs.
D. Prevent SSL VPN users from being logged out because of high network latency.

QUESTION 7

Which of the following conditions must be met in order for a web browser to trust a web server certificate signed by a third-party CA?

A. The public key of the web server certificate must be installed on the browser.
B. The web-server certificate must be installed on the browser.
C. The CA certificate that signed the web-server certificate must be installed on the browser.
D. The private key of the CA certificate that signed the browser certificate must be installed on the browser.

QUESTION 8

When using SD-WAN, how do you configure the next-hop gateway address for a member interface so that FortiGate can forward Internet traffic?

A. It must be configured in a static route using the **sdwan** virtual interface.

B. It must be provided in the SD-WAN member interface configuration.

C. It must be configured in a policy-route using the **sdwan** virtual interface.

D. It must be learned automatically through a dynamic routing protocol.

QUESTION 9

Which of the following services can be inspected by the DLP profile? (Choose three.)

A. NFS
B. FTP
C. IMAP
D. CIFS
E. HTTP-POST

QUESTION 10

Which of the following statements describe WMI polling mode for the FSSO collector agent? (Choose two.)

A. The **NetSessionEnum** function is used to track user logoffs.
B. WMI polling can increase bandwidth usage in large networks.
C. The collector agent uses a Windows API to query DCs for user logins.
D. The collector agent do not need to search any security event logs.

QUESTION 11

You are configuring the root FortiGate to implement the security fabric. You are configuring port10 to communicate with a downstream FortiGate. View the default **Edit Interface** in the exhibit below:

When configuring the root FortiGate to communicate with a downstream FortiGate, which settings are required to be configured? (Choose two.)

A. **Device detection** enabled.
B. **Administrative Access: FortiTelemetry**.
C. **IP/Network Mask**.
D. **Role: Security Fabric**.

QUESTION 12

What FortiGate components are tested during the hardware test? (Choose three.)

A. Administrative access
B. HA heartbeat
C. CPU
D. Hard disk
E. Network interfaces

QUESTION 13

Which statements correctly describe transparent mode operation? (Choose three.)

A. All interfaces of the transparent mode FortiGate device must be on different IP subnets.
B. Ethernet packets are forwarded based on destination MAC addresses, not IP addresses.
C. The transparent FortiGate is visible to network hosts in an IP traceroute.
D. It permits inline traffic inspection and firewalling without changing the IP scheme of the network.
E. FortiGate acts as transparent bridge and forwards traffic at Layer 2.

QUESTION 14

View the exhibit.

Which of the following statements are correct? (Choose two.)

A. This setup requires at least two firewall policies with the action set to IPsec.

B. Dead peer detection must be disabled to support this type of IPsec setup.

C. The **TunnelB** route is the primary route for reaching the remote site. The **TunnelA** route is used only if the **TunnelB** VPN is down.

D. This is a redundant IPsec setup.

QUESTION 15

Which one of the following processes is involved in updating IPS from FortiGuard?

A. FortiGate IPS update requests are sent using UDP port 443.

B. Protocol decoder update requests are sent to `service.fortiguard.net`.

C. IPS signature update requests are sent to `update.fortiguard.net`.

D. IPS engine updates can only be obtained using push updates.

QUESTION 16

How does FortiGate select the central SNAT policy that is applied to a TCP session?

A. It selects the SNAT policy specified in the configuration of the outgoing interface.
B. It selects the first matching central SNAT policy, reviewing from top to bottom.
C. It selects the central SNAT policy with the lowest priority.
D. It selects the SNAT policy specified in the configuration of the firewall policy that matches the traffic.

QUESTION 17

Which of the following conditions are required for establishing an IPSec VPN between two FortiGate devices? (Choose two.)

A. If XAuth is enabled as a server in one peer, it must be enabled as a client in the other peer.
B. If the VPN is configured as route-based, there must be at least one firewall policy with the action set to **IPSec**.
C. If the VPN is configured as **DialUp User** in one peer, it must be configured as either **Static IP Address** or **Dynamic DNS** in the other peer.
D. If the VPN is configured as a policy-based in one peer, it must also be configured as policy-based in the other peer.

QUESTION 18

Which of the following statements about converse mode are true? (Choose two.)

A. FortiGate stops sending files to FortiSandbox for inspection.
B. FortiGate stops doing RPF checks over incoming packets.
C. Administrators cannot change the configuration.
D. Administrators can access the FortiGate only through the console port.

QUESTION 19

View the exhibit.

```
192.168.2.1 - PuTTY                                    ?    X
login as: admin
Local-FortiGate #
Local-FortiGate # config vdom

Local-FortiGate (vdom) # edit root
current vf=root:0

Local-FortiGate (root) # config system global

command parse error before 'global'
Command fail. Return code 1

Local-FortiGate (root) #
```

Why is the administrator getting the error shown in the exhibit?

A. The administrator must first enter the command `edit global`.

B. The administrator `admin` does not have the privileges required to configure global settings.

C. The global settings cannot be configured from the `root` VDOM context.

D. The command `config system global` does not exist in FortiGate.

QUESTION 20

Examine the network diagram and the existing FGTI routing table shown in the exhibit, and then answer the following question:

An administrator has added the following static route on **FGTI**.

Since the change, the new static route is not showing up in the routing table. Given the information provided, which of the following describes the cause of this problem?

A. The new route's destination subnet overlaps an existing route.

B. The new route's **Distance** value should be higher than 10.

C. The **Gateway** IP address is not in the same subnet as **port1**.

D. The **Priority** is 0, which means that this route will remain inactive.

QUESTION 21

Which configuration objects can be selected for the **Source** field of a firewall policy? (Choose two.)

A. Firewall service
B. User or user group
C. IP Pool
D. FQDN address

QUESTION 22

View the exhibit.

Which users and user groups are allowed access to the network through captive portal?

A. Users and groups defined in the firewall policy.
B. Only individual users – not groups – defined in the captive portal configuration
C. Groups defined in the captive portal configuration
D. All users

QUESTION 23

NGFW mode allows policy-based configuration for most inspection rules. Which security profile's configuration does not change when you enable policy-based inspection?

A. Web filtering
B. Antivirus
C. Web proxy
D. Application control

QUESTION 24

During the digital verification process, comparing the original and fresh hash results satisfies which security requirement?

A. Authentication.
B. Data integrity.
C. Non-repudiation.
D. Signature verification.

QUESTION 25

An administration wants to throttle the total volume of SMTP sessions to their email server. Which of the following DoS sensors can be used to achieve this?

A. tcp_port_scan
B. ip_dst_session
C. udp_flood

D. ip_src_session

QUESTION 26

Why must you use aggressive mode when a local FortiGate IPSec gateway hosts multiple dialup tunnels?

A. In aggressive mode, the remote peers are able to provide their peer IDs in the first message.
B. FortiGate is able to handle NATed connections only in aggressive mode.
C. FortiClient only supports aggressive mode.
D. Main mode does not support XAuth for user authentication.

QUESTION 27

Examine this output from a debug flow:

```
id=20085 trace_id=1 func=print_pkt_detail line=5363 msg="vd-root received a packet(proto=1,
10.0.1.10:1->10.200.1.254:2048)
from port3. type=8, code=0, id=1, seq=33."
id=20085 trace_id=1 func=init_ip_session_common line=5519 msg="allocate a new session=00000340"
id=20085 trace_id=1 func=vf_ip_route_input_common line=2583 msg="find a route: flag=04000000 gw=10.200.1.254
port1"
id=20085 trace_id=1 func=fw_forward_handler line=586 msg="Denied by forward policy check (policy 0)"
```

Why did the FortiGate drop the packet?

A. The next-hop IP address is unreachable.
B. It failed the RPF check.
C. It matched an explicitly configured firewall policy with the action **DENY**.
D. It matched the default implicit firewall policy.

QUESTION 28

View the exhibit:

```
FortiGate # diagnose sniffer packet any "port 80" 4
interfaces=[any]
filters=[port 80]
11.510058 port3 in 10.0.1.10.49255 -> 10.200.1.254.80: syn 697263124
11.760531 port3 in 10.0.1.10.49256 -> 10.200.1.254.80: syn 868017830
14.505371 port3 in 10.0.1.10.49255 -> 10.200.1.254.80: syn 697263124
11.755510 port3 in 10.0.1.10.49256 -> 10.200.1.254.80: syn 868017830
```

The client cannot connect to the HTTP web server. The administrator ran the FortiGate built-in sniffer and got the following output:

What should be done next to troubleshoot the problem?

A. Run a sniffer in the web server.
B. Execute another sniffer in the FortiGate, this time with the filter "host 10.0.1.10".
C. Capture the traffic using an external sniffer connected to port1.
D. Execute a debug flow.

QUESTION 29

Which of the following statements about policy-based IPsec tunnels are true? (Choose two.)

A. They can be configured in both NAT/Route and transparent operation modes.
B. They support L2TP-over-IPsec.
C. They require two firewall policies: one for each directions of traffic flow.
D. They support GRE-over-IPsec.

QUESTION 30

An employee connects to the https://example.com on the Internet using a web browser. The web server's certificate was signed by a private internal CA. The FortiGate that is inspecting this traffic is configured for full SSL inspection.

This exhibit shows the configuration settings for the SSL/SSH inspection profile that is applied to the policy that is invoked in this instance. All other settings are set to defaults. No certificates have been imported into FortiGate. View the exhibit and answer the question that follows.

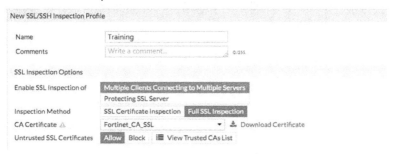

Which certificate is presented to the employee's web browser?

A. The web server's certificate.
B. The user's personal certificate signed by a private internal CA.
C. A certificate signed by Fortinet_CA_SSL.
D. A certificate signed by Fortinet_CA_Untrusted.

QUESTION 31

An administrator is attempting to allow access to `https://fortinet.com` through a firewall policy that is configured with a web filter and an SSL inspection profile configured for deep inspection. Which of the following are possible actions to eliminate the certificate error generated by deep inspection? (Choose two.)

A. Implement firewall authentication for all users that need access to `fortinet.com`.

B. Manually install the FortiGate deep inspection certificate as a trusted CA.

C. Configure `fortinet.com` access to bypass the IPS engine.

D. Configure an SSL-inspection exemption for `fortinet.com`.

QUESTION 32

How does FortiGate verify the login credentials of a remote LDAP user?

A. FortiGate regenerates the algorithm based on the login credentials and compares it to the algorithm stored on the LDAP server.

B. FortiGate sends the user-entered credentials to the LDAP server for authentication.

C. FortiGate queries the LDAP server for credentials.

D. FortiGate queries its own database for credentials.

QUESTION 33

Which action can be applied to each filter in the application control profile?

A. Block, monitor, warning, and quarantine
B. Allow, monitor, block and learn
C. Allow, block, authenticate, and warning
D. Allow, monitor, block, and quarantine

QUESTION 34

View the exhibit.

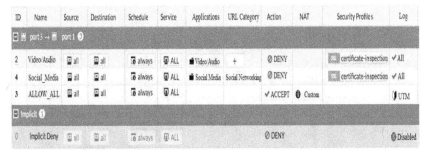

ID	Name	Source	Destination	Schedule	Service	Applications	URL Category	Action	NAT	Security Profiles	Log
🖻 📓 port3 → 📓 port1 ⊗											
2	Video/Audio	📃 all	📃 all	ⓞ always	🗊 ALL	■ Video/Audio +		⊘ DENY		certificate-inspection ✔ All	
4	Social_Media	📃 all	📃 all	ⓞ always	🗊 ALL	■ Social Media Social Networking		⊘ DENY		certificate-inspection ✔ All	
3	ALLOW_ALL	📃 all	📃 all	ⓞ always	🗊 ALL			✔ ACCEPT	❶ Custom		🜲 UTM
🖻 Implicit ❶											
0	Implicit Deny	📃 all	📃 all	ⓞ always	🗊 ALL			⊘ DENY			⊗ Disabled

Based on the configuration shown in the exhibit, what statements about application control behavior are true? (Choose two.)

A. Access to all unknown applications will be allowed.
B. Access to browser-based **Social.Media** applications will be blocked.
C. Access to mobile social media applications will be blocked.
D. Access to all applications in **Social.Media** category will be blocked.

QUESTION 35

HTTP Public Key Pinning (HPKP) can be an obstacle to implementing full SSL inspection. What solutions could resolve this problem? (Choose two.)

A. Enable **Allow Invalid SSL Certificates** for the relevant security profile.

B. Change web browsers to one that does not support HPKP.

C. Exempt those web sites that use HPKP from full SSL inspection.

D. Install the CA certificate (that is required to verify the web server certificate) stores of users' computers.

QUESTION 36

View the exhibit.
What does this raw log indicate? (Choose two.)

```
date=2018-01-30 time=07:21:49 logid="0316013057" type="utm" subtype="webfilter"
eventtype="ftgd_blk" level="warning" vd="root" logtime=1517325709 policyid=1
sessionid=15332 srcip=10.0.1.20 scrport=59538 srcintf="port3" srcintfrole="undefined"
dstip=208.91.112.55 dstport=80 dstintf="port1" dstintfrole="undefined" proto=6
service="HTTP" hostname="lavito.tk" profile="Category-block-and-warning" action="blocked"
reqtype="direct" url="/" sentbyte=140 rcvdbyte=0 direction="outgoing" msg="URL belongs
a category with warnings enabled" method="domain" cat=0 catdesc="Unrated" crscore=30
crlevel="high"
```

ID	Name	From	To
2	IPS	port1	port3
1	Full_Access	port3	port1
0	Implicit Deny	☐ any	☐ any

A. FortiGate blocked the traffic.

B. `type` indicates that a security event was recorded.

C. `10.0.1.20` is the IP address for `lavito.tk`.

D. `policyid` indicates that traffic went through the **IPS** firewall policy.

QUESTION 37

Which of the following statements are true when using WPAD with the DHCP discovery method? (Choose two.)

A. If the DHCP method fails, browsers will try the DNS method.
B. The browser needs to be preconfigured with the DHCP server's IP address.
C. The browser sends a DHCPONFORM request to the DHCP server.
D. The DHCP server provides the PAC file for download.

QUESTION 38

Examine the routing database shown in the exhibit, and then answer the following question:

```
FGT1 # get router info routing-table database
Codes: K - kernel, C - connected, S - static, R - RIP, B - BGP
       O - OSPF, IA - OSPF inter area
       N1 - OSPF NSSA external type 1, N2 - OSPF NSSA external type 2
       E1 - OSPF external type 1, E2 - OSPF external type 2
       i - IS-IS, L1 - IS-IS level-1, L2 - IS-IS level-2, ia - IS-IS inter area
       > - selected route, * - FIB route, p - stale info

S     *> 0.0.0.0/0 [10/0] via 172.20.121.2, port1, [20/0]
      *>            [10/0] via 10.0.0.2, port2, [30/0]
S        0.0.0.0/0 [20/0] via 192.168.15.2, port3, [10/0]
C     *> 10.0.0.0/24 is directly connected, port2
S        172.13.24.0/24 [10/0] is directly connected, port4
C     *> 172.20.121.0/24 is directly connected, port1
S     *> 192.167.1.0/24 [10/0] via 10.0.0.2, port2
C     *> 192.168.15.0/24 is directly connected, port3
```

Which of the following statements are correct? (Choose two.)

A. The **port3** default route has the highest distance.
B. The **port3** default route has the lowest metric.
C. There will be eight routes active in the routing table.
D. The **port1** and **port2** default routes are active in the routing table.

QUESTION 39

If traffic matches a DLP filter with the action set to **Quarantine IP Address**, what action does FortiGate take?

A. It notifies the administrator by sending an email.
B. It provides a DLP block replacement page with a link to download the file.
C. It blocks all future traffic for that IP address for a configured interval.
D. It archives the data for that IP address.

QUESTION 40

Which of the following statements about the FSSO collector agent timers is true?

A. The **workstation verify interval** is used to periodically check of a workstation is still a domain member.
B. The **IP address change verify interval** monitors the server IP address where the collector agent is installed, and the updates the collector agent configuration if it changes.
C. The **user group cache expiry** is used to age out the monitored groups.
D. The **dead entry timeout interval** is used to age out entries with an unverified status.

QUESTION 41

A FortiGate device has multiple VDOMs. Which statement about an administrator account configured with the default **prof_admin** profile is true?

A. It can create administrator accounts with access to the same VDOM.
B. It cannot have access to more than one VDOM.
C. It can reset the password for the **admin** account.
D. It can upgrade the firmware on the FortiGate device.

QUESTION 42

Which of the following features is supported by web filter in flow-based inspection mode with NGFW mode set to profile-based?

A. FortiGuard Quotas
B. Static URL
C. Search engines
D. Rating option

QUESTION 43

Examine the exhibit, which contains a virtual IP and firewall policy configuration.

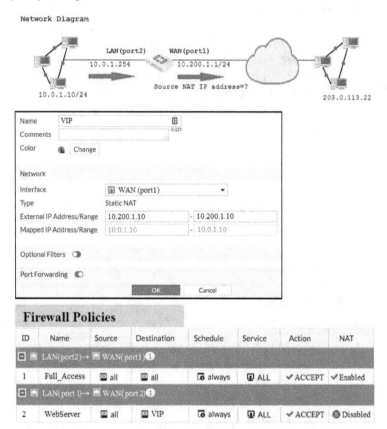

Network Diagram

The WAN (port1) interface has the IP address `10.200.1.1/24`. The LAN (port2) interface has the IP address `10.0.1.254/24`.
The first firewall policy has NAT enabled on the outgoing interface address. The second firewall policy is configured with a VIP as the destination address. Which IP address will be used to source NAT the Internet traffic coming from a workstation with the IP address `10.0.1.10/24`?

A. 10.200.1.10

B. Any available IP address in the WAN (port1) subnet
10.200.1.0/24

C. 10.200.1.1

D. 10.0.1.254

QUESTION 44

By default, when logging to disk, when does FortiGate delete
logs?

A. 30 days
B. 1 year
C. Never
D. 7 days

QUESTION 45

Examine the exhibit, which contains a session diagnostic
output.

Which of the following statements about the session diagnostic
output is true?

```
session info: proto=6 proto_state=01 duration=26 expire=3594 timeout=3600 flags=00000000 sockflag=
00000000 sockport=0 av_idx=0 use=4
origin-shaper=
reply-shaper=
per_ip_shaper=
ha_id=0 policy-dir=0 tunnel=/ vlan_cos=0/255
state=may_dirty
statistic(bytes/packets/allow_err): org=1490/14/1 reply=10479/13/1 tuples=2
tx speed (Bps/kbps):56/0 rx speed(Bps/kbps):397/3
orgin->sink: org pre->post, reply pre->post dev=5->3/3->5 gwy=10.200.1.254/10.0.1.10
hook=post dir=org act=snat 10.0.1.10:60267->52.84.125.124:443(10.200.1.100:60267)
hook=pre dir=reply act=dnat 52.84.125.124:443->10.200.1.100:60267(10.0.1.10:60267)
pos/ (before,after) 0/(0,0), 0/(0,0)
misc=0 policy_id=1 auth_info=0 chk_client_info=0 vd=0
serial=00009bd8 tos=ff/ff app_list=0 app=0 url_cat=0
dd_type=0 dd_mode=0
total session 129
```

A. The session is in ESTABLISHED state.

B. The session is in `LISTEN` state.

C. The session is in `TIME_WAIT` state.

D. The session is in `CLOSE_WAIT` state.

QUESTION 46

Which of the following statements about backing up logs from the CLI and downloading logs from the GUI are true? (Choose two.)

A. Log downloads from the GUI are limited to the current filter view

B. Log backups from the CLI cannot be restored to another FortiGate.

C. Log backups from the CLI can be configured to upload to FTP as a scheduled time

D. Log downloads from the GUI are stored as LZ4 compressed files.

QUESTION 47

Examine the network diagram shown in the exhibit, then answer the following question:

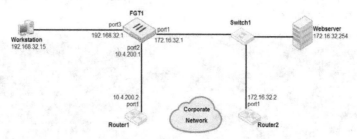

Which one of the following routes is the best candidate route for FGT1 to route traffic from the Workstation to the Web server?

A. 172.16.0.0/16 [50/0] via 10.4.200.2, port2 [5/0]

B. 0.0.0.0/0 [20/0] via 10.4.200.2, port2
C. 10.4.200.0/30 is directly connected, port2
D. 172.16.32.0/24 is directly connected, port1

QUESTION 48

A team manager has decided that while some members of the team need access to particular website, the majority of the team does not. Which configuration option is the most effective option to support this request?

A. Implement a web filter category override for the specified website.
B. Implement web filter authentication for the specified website
C. Implement web filter quotas for the specified website.
D. Implement DNS filter for the specified website.

QUESTION 49

You have tasked to design a new IPsec deployment with the
    following criteria: There are two HQ sues that all satellite offices must connect to
    The satellite offices do not need to communicate directly
    with other satellite offices No dynamic routing will be used
    The design should minimize the number of tunnels being configured.

Which topology should be used to satisfy all of the requirements?

A. Partial mesh
B. Hub-and-spoke
C. Fully meshed
D. Redundant

QUESTION 50

Which of the following statements is true regarding SSL VPN settings for an SSL VPN portal?

A. By default, FortiGate uses WINS servers to resolve names.
B. By default, the SSL VPN portal requires the installation of a client's certificate.
C. By default, split tunneling is enabled.
D. By default, the admin GUI and SSL VPN portal use the same HTTPS port.

QUESTION 51

An administrator has configured the following settings:

```
config system settings
set ses-denied-traffic enable
end

config system global
set block-session-timer 30
end
```

What does the configuration do? (Choose two.)

A. Reduces the amount of logs generated by denied traffic.
B. Enforces device detection on all interfaces for 30 minutes.
C. Blocks denied users for 30 minutes.
D. Creates a session for traffic being denied.

QUESTION 52

An administrator observes that the port1 interface cannot be configured with an IP address. What can be the reasons for that? (Choose three.)

A. The interface has been configured for one-arm sniffer.
B. The interface is a member of a virtual wire pair.
C. The operation mode is transparent.
D. The interface is a member of a zone.
E. Captive portal is enabled in the interface.

QUESTION 53

Which is the correct description of a hash result as it relates to digital certificates?

A. A unique value used to verify the input data
B. An output value that is used to identify the person or deduce that authored the input data.
C. An obfuscation used to mask the input data.
D. An encrypted output value used to safe-guard the input data

QUESTION 54

Examine the exhibit, which shows the partial output of an IKE real-time debug.

```
ike 0: comes 172.20.187.114:500->172.20.186.222:500,ifindex=2....
ike 0: IKEv1 exchange=Identity Protection id=4497f0b077c742b5/0000000000000000 len=296
ike 0:4497f0b077c742b5/0000000000000000:8: responder: main mode get 1st message...

ike 0:4497f0b077c742b5/0000000000000000:8: SA proposal chosen, matched gateway Remote
ike 0: found Remote 172.20.186.222 2 -> 172.20.187.114:500

ike 0:Remote:8: sent IKE msg (ident_r1send): 172.20.186.222:500->172.20.187.114:500, len=160
ike 0: comes 172.20.187.114:500->172.20.186.222:500,ifindex=2....
ike 0:Remote:8: responder:main mode get 2nd message...
....
ike 0:Remote:8: sent IKE msg (ident_r2send): 172.20.186.222:500->172.20.187.114:500, len=292
ike 0:Remote:8: ISAKMP SA 4497f0b077c742b5/fbbb59b259a0fc3e key 24:DCD18FBE7CFA138E27B06F
ike 0: comes 172.20.187.114:500->172.20.186.222:500,ifindex=2....
ike 0:Remote:8: responder: main mode get 3rd message...
...
ike 0:Remote:8: PSK authentication succeeded
ike 0:Remote:8: authentication OK
ike 0:Remote:8: established IKE SA 4497f0b077c742b5/fbbb59b259a0fc3e
```

Which of the following statement about the output is true?
A. The VPN is configured to use pre-shared key authentication.
B. Extended authentication (XAuth) was successful.
C. Remote is the host name of the remote IPsec peer.
D. Phase 1 went down.

QUESTION 55

Examine the network diagram shown in the exhibit, and then answer the following question:

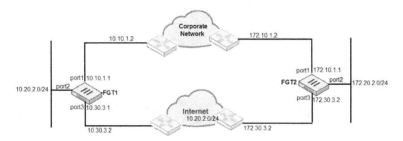

A firewall administrator must configure equal cost multipath (ECMP) routing on FGT1 to ensure both port1 and port3 links are used at the same time for all traffic destined for 172.20.2.0/24. Which of the following static routes will satisfy this requirement on FGT1? (Choose two.)

A. 172.20.2.0/24 (1/0) via 10.10.1.2, port1 [0/0]

B. 172.20.2.0/24 (25/0) via 10.10.3.2, port3 [5/0]

C. 172.20.2.0/24 (1/150) via 10.10.3.2, port3 [10/0]

D. 172.20.2.0/24 (1/150) via 10.30.3.2, port3 [10/0]

QUESTION 56

Examine this FortiGate configuration:

```
config system global

    set av-failopen pass

end

config system global

    set av-failopen pass

end
```

Examine the output of the following debug command:
Based on the diagnostic outputs above, how is the FortiGate handling the traffic for new sessions that require inspection?

A. It is allowed, but with no inspection
B. It is allowed and inspected as long as the inspection is flow based
C. It is dropped.
D. It is allowed and inspected, as long as the only inspection required is antivirus.

QUESTION 57

When using WPAD DNS method, which FQDN format do browsers use to query the DNS server?

A. `srv_proxy.<local-domain>/wpad.dat`
B. `srv_tcp.wpad.<local-domain>`
C. `wpad.<local-domain>`
D. `proxy.<local-domain>.wpad`

QUESTION 58

Examine the IPS sensor configuration shown in the exhibit, and then answer the question below.

IPS Sensor

Name: WINDOWS_SERVERS   [View IPS Signatures]

Comments: 0 255

IPS Signatures

+ Add Signatures   Delete   Edit IP Exemptions

Name	Exempt IPs	Severity	Target	Service	OS	Action	Packet Logging
No matching entries found							

IPS Filters

+ Add Filter   Edit Filter   Delete

Filter Details	Action	Packet Logging
Location:server OS:Windows	⊘ Block	○

Apply

Forward Traffic Logs

↻ ⬇ ⊕ Add Filter

#	Date/Time	Source	Destination	Application Name	Result	Policy
1	10:09:03	10.200.1.254	10.200.1.200	HTTPS	1.30kB/2.65 kB	2(Web-Server-Access-IPS)
2	10:09:03	10.200.1.254	10.200.1.200	HTTPS	1.30kB/2.65 kB	2(Web-Server-Access-IPS)
3	10:09:02	10.200.1.254	10.200.1.200	HTTPS	1.30kB/2.65 kB	2(Web-Server-Access-IPS)
4	10:09:02	10.200.1.254	10.200.1.200	HTTPS	1.30kB/2.65 kB	2(Web-Server-Access-IPS)
5	10:09:01	10.200.1.254	10.200.1.200	HTTPS	1.30kB/2.65 kB	2(Web-Server-Access-IPS)
6	10.08.59	10.200.1.254	10.200.1.200	HTTPS	1.30kB/2.65 kB	2(Web-Server-Access-IPS)
7	10:08:57	10.200.1.254	10.200.1.200	HTTPS	1.30kB/2.65 kB	2(Web-Server-Access-IPS)
8	10:08:57	10.200.1.254	10.200.1.200	HTTPS	1.30kB/2.65 kB	2(Web-Server-Access-IPS)
9	10:08:57	10.200.1.254	10.200.1.200	HTTPS	1.30kB/2.65 kB	2(Web-Server-Access-IPS)
10	10:08:57	10.200.1.254	10.200.1.200	HTTPS	1.30kB/2.65 kB	2(Web-Server-Access-IPS)

An administrator has configured the WINDOS_SERVERS IPS sensor in an attempt to determine whether the influx of HTTPS traffic is an attack attempt or not. After applying the IPS sensor, FortiGate is still not generating any IPS logs for the HTTPS traffic. What is a possible reason for this?

A. The IPS filter is missing the Protocol: HTTPS option.
B. The HTTPS signatures have not been added to the sensor.
C. A DoS policy should be used, instead of an IPS sensor.
D. A DoS policy should be used, instead of an IPS sensor.
E. The firewall policy is not using a full SSL inspection profile.

QUESTION 59

What types of traffic and attacks can be blocked by a web application firewall (WAF) profile? (Choose three.)

A. Traffic to botnetservers
B. Traffic to inappropriate web sites
C. Server information disclosure attacks
D. Credit card data leaks
E. SQL injection attacks

QUESTION 60

Examine this PAC file configuration.

```
function FindProxyForURL (url, host) {
  if (shExpMatch (url, "*.fortinet.com/*")) {
    return "DIRECT";}
  if (isInNet (host, "172.25.120.0", "255.255.255.0")) {
    return "PROXY" altproxy.corp.com: 8060";}
  return "PROXY proxy.corp.com: 8090";
  }
```

Which of the following statements are true? (Choose two.)

A. Browsers can be configured to retrieve this PAC file from the FortiGate.
B. Any web request to the 172.25.120.0/24 subnet is allowed to bypass the proxy.
C. All requests not made to Fortinet.com or the 172.25.120.0/24 subnet, have to go through altproxy.corp.com: 8060.
D. Any web request fortinet.com is allowed to bypass the proxy.

QUESTION 61

Which statements best describe auto discovery VPN (ADVPN).
(Choose two.)

A. It requires the use of dynamic routing protocols so that spokes can learn the routes to other spokes.
B. ADVPN is only supported with IKEv2.
C. Tunnels are negotiated dynamically between spokes.
D. Every spoke requires a static tunnel to be configured to other spokes so that phase 1 and phase 2 proposals are defined in advance.

QUESTION 62

An administrator needs to create an SSL-VPN connection for accessing an internal server using the bookmark Port Forward. What step is required for this configuration?

A. Configure an SSL VPN realm for clients to use the port forward bookmark.
B. Configure the client application to forward IP traffic through FortiClient.
C. Configure the virtual IP address to be assigned t the SSL VPN users.
D. Configure the client application to forward IP traffic to a Java applet proxy.

QUESTION 63

Which statements are true regarding firewall policy NAT using the outgoing interface IP address with fixed port disabled? (Choose two.)

A. This is known as many-to-one NAT.
B. Source IP is translated to the outgoing interface IP.
C. Connections are tracked using source port and source MAC address.
D. Port address translation is not used.

ANSWERS

1. Correct Answer: B
2. Correct Answer: AC
3. Correct Answer: BC
4. Correct Answer: C
5. Correct Answer: B
6. Correct Answer: AD
7. Correct Answer: C
8. Correct Answer: A
9. Correct Answer: BCE
10. Correct Answer: BC
11. Correct Answer: BC
12. Correct Answer: CDE
13. Correct Answer: BDE
14. Correct Answer: CD
15. Correct Answer: C
16. Correct Answer: B
17. Correct Answer: BC
18. Correct Answer: AB
19. Correct Answer: C
20. Correct Answer: C
21. Correct Answer: BC
22. Correct Answer: C
23. Correct Answer: C
24. Correct Answer: D
25. Correct Answer: A
26. Correct Answer: A
27. Correct Answer: D
28. Correct Answer: C
29. Correct Answer: AB
30. Correct Answer: A
31. Correct Answer: BD
32. Correct Answer: B
33. Correct Answer: D
34. Correct Answer: BD
35. Correct Answer: BC

Reference: https://cookbook.fortinet.com/exempting-

36. Correct Answer: BD
37. Correct Answer: AC
38. Correct Answer: AD
39. Correct Answer: C
40. Correct Answer: D
41. Correct Answer: C
42. Correct Answer: D
43. Correct Answer: C
44. Correct Answer: D
45. Correct Answer: A
46. Correct Answer: BC
47. Correct Answer: D
48. Correct Answer: A
49. Correct Answer: B
50. Correct Answer: D
51. Correct Answer: CD
52. Correct Answer: ABC
53. Correct Answer: A
54. Correct Answer: A
55. Correct Answer: CD
56. Correct Answer: A
57. Correct Answer: C
58. Correct Answer: E
59. Correct Answer: ACE
60. Correct Answer: AD
61. Correct Answer: AC
62. Correct Answer: D
63. Correct Answer: AB